Published by Weigl Publishers Inc.
350 5th Avenue, Suite 3304, PMB 6G
New York, NY 10118-0069

Website: www.weigl.com

All of the Internet URLs given in the book were valid at the time of publication. However, due to the
dynamic nature of the Internet, some addresses may have changed, or sites may have ceased to exist
since publication. While the author and publisher regret any inconvenience this may cause readers,
no responsibility for any such changes can be accepted by either the author or the publisher.

Library of Congress Cataloging-in-Publication Data

Lambert, Deborah.
 Verbs / Deborah Lambert.
     p. cm. -- (Learning to write)
 Includes webliography and index.
 ISBN 978-1-60596-044-9 (hard cover : alk. paper) -- ISBN 978-1-60596-045-6 (soft cover : alk.
paper)
 1. English language--Verb--Juvenile literature. I. Title.
 PE1271.L36 2009
 428.2--dc22

                         2009001949

Printed in China
1 2 3 4 5 6 7 8 9 0 13 12 11 10 09

Editor: Deborah G. Lambert
Design: Terry Paulhus

Photograph Credits

Weigl acknowledges Getty images as its primary image supplier for this title.

Other photograph credits include: **Photos.com:** page 3; **MODIS Rapid Response Team, NASA God-
dard Space Flight Center Images captured by the MODIS instrument on board the Terra or Aqua
satellite:** page 6; **U. S. Fish and Wildlife Service:** page 16.

All of the internet URLs given in the book were valid at the time of publication. However, due to the
dynamic nature of the internet, some addresses may have changed, or sites may have ceased to exist
since publication. While the author and publisher regret any inconvenience this may cause readers,
no responsibility for any such changes can be accepted by either the author or the publisher.

Every reasonable effort has been made to trace ownership and to obtain permission to reprint
copyright material. The publishers would be pleased to have any errors or omissions brought
to their attention so that they may be corrected in subsequent printings.

Table of Contents

4   What is a Verb?

6   Identifying Types of Verbs

8   Learning about Action Verbs

10   Learning about Linking Verbs

12   Learning about Helping Verbs

14   Where Do They Belong?

16   Using Verbs to Create Sentences

18   Tools for Learning about Verbs

20   Put Your Knowledge to Use

22   Other Parts of Speech

23   Further Research

24   Glossary/Index

What is a Verb?

A verb is a part of speech that describes what a **noun** or **pronoun** is doing in a sentence. Some examples of verbs are shaded red in the following paragraph about plant and animal life in the Sahara **Desert**. The Sahara Desert is the largest desert in the world. It is found in the northern part of Africa.

There is a surprising amount of life in the Sahara Desert. Many of the plants in the Sahara live for only a few days. Their seeds then lie in the ground until the next rainfall, when the cycle begins again. Other plants have long roots that go deep into the ground for water.

Many of the animals living in the Sahara are nocturnal. This means they are most active at night, when the air is cooler.

To read more about the Sahara Desert, go to **http://geography.howstuffworks.com/africa/ the-sahara-desert4.htm.**

Look for other examples of verbs being used on this site to tell what is happening in the Sahara Desert.

Finding the Verbs

The following paragraphs talk about the Mississippi River. This river is the largest river in North America. What verbs have been used to describe what is taking place in or near that river? Make a list of these verbs in your notebook.

The Mississippi River begins its journey in Minnesota and empties into the Gulf of Mexico from the Louisiana coast. It supplies water to millions of people. People and animals need the river for drinking water. Farmers use it to water their crops. No wonder this river is often called the Mighty Mississippi!

Before there were cars and trains, many people used canoes to travel on the Mississippi River. Aboriginal peoples, and later, Europeans, settled along its banks.

Identifying Types of Verbs

There are three basic types of verbs in the English language. These types include *action, linking,* and *helping* verbs.

Action verbs describe the action being done by the noun or pronoun in a sentence. A few examples of these verbs include *write, walk, sit, think,* and *dream.*

Linking verbs link the noun or pronoun with the rest of the sentence. A few examples of these verbs include *am, are, is, be, was,* and *were.*

Helping verbs are found in front of action verbs and linking verbs. Some examples of helping verbs include *can, may, will, has,* and *have.*

See how these types of verbs have been used in this paragraph about the Great Lakes.

The Great Lakes contain a large amount of Earth's fresh water. These lakes are home to many plants and animals. Aboriginal Peoples have lived around these lakes for thousands of years.

In the paragraph, the word "contain" is an action verb. The word "are" is a linking verb, and "have" is the helping verb for the action verb "lived."

Selecting Types of Verbs

Verbs have been used in this paragraph about Mauna Loa. Mauna Loa is the largest volcano on Earth. It is so large that it covers half the island of Hawai'i. Find the verbs in the paragraph, and list them in your notebook.

*Mauna Loa is an active volcano. This means that it **erupts** often. Some past eruptions have covered areas the size of 100 football fields with **lava**. Other eruptions have destroyed villages and towns. The people who lived in these villages and towns had time to leave their homes safely. Today, some people still live near Mauna Loa.*

To learn more about Mauna Loa go to **www.soest.hawaii.edu/GG/ HCV/maunaloa.html**. Look for more verbs on this website, and add them to your list.

Learning about Action Verbs

Action verbs are also known as doing verbs. They describe the action being done by the noun or pronoun in a sentence.

Study the action verbs that are shaded red in this paragraph about the yak. The yak is one of the few animals that live on Mount Everest, one of the highest mountains on Earth. Very few living things are able to survive there.

To make sure that a verb in a sentence is an action verb, you must ask yourself this question.

> *Does this verb describe something I can do?*

The verb to which you can answer "yes" is the action verb. Now, read the following paragraph. Try asking if each of the words that are shaded red is something you can do. If the answer is yes, then you know that they are action verbs.

Yaks are one of the few mammals that live on Mount Everest. They are important to the humans who live on the mountain. They are also important to humans who visit Mount Everest. Yaks carry heavy loads. Sometimes, these loads weigh more than 300 pounds (136 kilograms).

Identifying Action Verbs

There are action verbs in the following legend about the Yeti. The Yeti, also called the Abominable Snowman, is said to live on Mount Everest. Read these paragraphs, and make a list of the action verbs in your notebook.

There have been many stories told over the years about the Yeti. According to legend, the Yeti is a creature that is half-man and half-ape. In 1951, explorer Eric Shipton took photos of giant footprints in the snow. He claimed that these were the tracks of the Yeti. No one could prove whether this was true or not.

Over the past 50 years, other people claimed to have seen a creature like the Yeti on Mount Everest. The Yeti's legend continues to grow, but no one has been able to prove that the Yeti exists.

To read more about the Yeti, go to **http://cryptozoo.monstrous.com/ the_yeti.htm**. As you read, add more action verbs to your list.

Learning about Linking Verbs

Linking verbs link the noun or pronoun with the rest of the sentence. Some linking verbs are also called **being verbs**. These include *am*, *are*, *is*, *was*, *were*, *has*, *have*, and *be*.

In the following sentences about Angel Falls, one of the linking verbs has been shaded red. Make a list of the linking verbs in the other sentences. Use the list of linking verbs that is on this page to help you.

Angel Falls is the highest waterfall in the world.

Other than the indigenous peoples, Ruth Robertson and her team were the first humans to see Angel Falls.

There are plants near Angel Falls that cannot be found anywhere else on Earth.

Jimmie Angel was one of the first explorers to see Angel Falls.

Identifying Linking Verbs

Read the following sentences about the Great Barrier Reef. Make a list of all the linking verbs that are in these sentences.

The Great Barrier Reef is home to some of the most beautiful creatures in the world.

The clown and parrot are some of the fish found there.

The first people to discover the Great Barrier Reef were the **Aboriginal Australians.**

Matthew Flinders, a British explorer, was the first person to sail around the entire Australian continent. The Great Barrier Reef caused problems to many ship captains like him.

Now, go to **www.nationalgeographic.com/features/00/earthpulse/ reef/reef1_flash.html**. Make a list of some of the linking verbs used on this site. Which linking verbs are used most often?

Learning about Helping Verbs

Helping verbs are always followed by action or linking verbs in a sentence. They are never used by themselves. Some of the most common helping verbs are *has, have, had, will, may, would, should, can,* and *could.* Linking verbs that are being verbs can also act as helping verbs.

Look at some examples in this paragraph about plants found around Victoria Falls. The helping verbs are shaded red. The verbs they are helping are shaded blue.

How can you tell the difference between helping verbs and the being verbs that are also linking verbs? You can tell by checking to see whether any action verbs immediately follow the being verbs.

Examples of helping verbs are shaded red in this paragraph. The action or linking verbs they help are shaded blue.

Not all the plants at Victoria Falls have been there for long. Some were brought to Victoria Falls area by early European settlers. Many are known as pest plants. Lantana is a pretty plant, but it can spread quickly and poison cattle.

Identifying Helping Verbs

This paragraph is about some of the plants that are found in the Amazon rain forest. Most of the Amazon rain forest lies in the country of Brazil. It also **extends** into eight other South American countries.

Read the paragraph carefully. Then make a list of all the helping verbs you can find.

Indigenous peoples have lived in the Amazon rain forest for thousands of years. During that time, they have come to know many of the plants there and their uses. Some of what they know has spread to other parts of the world. For example, rubber taken from the Amazon's rubber trees is used in many places around the world.

Now, rewrite each sentence, changing the helping verbs to action verbs.

Where Do They Belong?

In learning to use verbs, you should be able to identify each type of verb when it is used. In this paragraph about traveling across the Sahara Desert, some verbs are shaded red.

For almost 2,000 years, camels were used to bring people and goods across the desert. Today, some people still use them to cross the desert. Many people also travel in trucks that are made for the desert. Crossing the desert can be dangerous. People who get lost may wait for days before they are found.

Each of the verbs shown belongs to one of the types talked about in this book. Some have been placed in the proper column in this chart.

VERBS		
Action	**Linking**	**Helping**
bring	are	were (used)

In which columns do the other verbs in the paragraph above belong?

Grouping Verbs

There are some verbs in this legend about Mount Kilimanjaro. Mount Kilimanjaro is the tallest mountain in Africa. In your notebook, draw a chart like the one on this page. Then, place each verb from this paragraph in the proper column. Three examples have been done for you.

When Johannes Rebmann first saw Mount Kilimanjaro, he was told that its top was covered with a strange white powder that looked like silver. The local people believed that the mountain was protected by spirits. They thought that these spirits would punish any person who tried to climb the mountain. Rebmann soon learned that the silver was snow. He also learned that the spirits were the **extreme** *cold. The local people still have great respect for the mountain. To them, it is the home of the gods.*

VERBS		
Action	**Linking**	**Helping**
saw	was	was (told)

Using Verbs to Create Sentences

Like nouns and pronouns, verbs are important parts of a sentence, paragraph, or story. Imagine trying to write a sentence, for example, without using verbs.

Study the use of verbs in the paragraph about animal life in the Great Lakes. These verbs are shaded red.

Use these same verbs to write your own sentences about some of the animals found near the Great Lakes. One has been done for you.

> Owls and squirrels are two animals found near the Great Lakes.

There are many types of animals in the Great Lakes. These animals compete with each other for food. Wolves, black bears, lynx, and moose live near Lakes Superior, Michigan, and Huron. Owls, squirrels, and white-tailed deer are found in the forests near the lower Great Lakes region. There are also many types of fish in the Great Lakes. These fish feed on the insects and plants that live in and around the water.

Creating Your Own Sentences Using Types of Verbs

Look at the image on this page. It is a picture of the blue-ringed octopus. This octopus is one of the creatures that is found in the Great Barrier Reef.

The blue-ringed octopus is one of the reef's deadliest creatures. If this octopus bites a person, this person will die after only a few minutes.

Use the Internet, or visit the library, to find out more information about the blue-ringed octopus. Then, write three sentences about how it lives, using the types of verbs explained in this book.

Tools for Learning about Verbs

What did you learn? Look at the topics in the "Skills" column. Compare them to the page number in the "Page" column. Review the content you learned about verbs by reading the "Content" column below.

SKILLS	CONTENT	PAGE
Defining a verb	Sahara Desert, Mississippi River	4–5
Identifying types of verbs	Great Lakes, Mauna Loa	6–7
Learning about action verbs	Yaks on Mount Everest, Yeti on Mount Everest	8–9
Learning about linking verbs	Angel Falls, Great Barrier Reef	10–11
Learning about helping verbs	Victoria Falls, plants in the Amazon rain forest	12–13
Grouping verbs according to type	Sahara Desert, Mount Kilimanjaro	14–15
Using verbs	Great Lakes, blue-ringed octopus in the Great Barrier Reef	16–17

Practice Writing Your Own Paragraphs Using Different Types of Verbs

These paragraphs describe how people live on two of the world's tallest mountains, Mount Everest and Mount Kilimanjaro.

Mount Everest is not an easy place to live. Many groups of people live there, but the Sherpas are the best-known people on this mountain. They live in small villages, where they farm the land and herd animals, such as goats and yaks.

As more visitors travel to Mount Everest, Sherpas have made their living as guides and porters.

The Chagga have lived around Mount Kilimanjaro for about 400 years. They use the land for farming. Some of the food they grow includes coffee, bananas, barley, wheat, and sugar. The Chagga also raise cattle and collect honey. They work as guides and porters as well.

1. Study these paragraphs carefully. Then, make a list of all the verbs that have been used to describe how both groups of people live on these mountains.

2. Use the verbs from the list to write a paragraph about how both groups of people live on these mountains.

Legends have been told about some of the natural wonders of the world. Two of these legends are about the Grand Canyon of Arizona and the Devil's Tower of Wyoming.

For a legend about the Grand Canyon, go to **http://grand-canyon-vacation-information.com/grand-canyon-indian-legend.html**.

A legend about the Devil's Tower, can be found at **www.angelfire.com/ca/Indian/DevilsTower.html**.

Read these legends. Then, in your own words, write a story about one of these legends using the types of verbs that you have learned in this book.

The following are pictures of the Grand Canyon and the Devil's Tower.

The Grand Canyon took six million years to be created. It is more than one mile (1.6 kilometers) deep and 277 miles (446 km) long.

The Devil's Tower is a sacred place for many American Indian groups, including the Lakota. It is about 5,112 feet (1.6 kilometers) high.

Use the Internet, or visit the library to find out more information about other natural wonders found in the United States. In your notebook, write a story about one of these natural wonders, using the types of verbs that you learned in this book.

You can start with some information about the Crater Lake found in Oregon at **www.nps.gov/crla**. The following are pictures of the Crater Lake in Oregon.

EXPANDED CHECKLIST

Reread your sentences, paragraphs, or stories to make sure that you have all of the following.

- ☑ Verbs that describe action

- ☑ Verbs that link nouns or pronouns to the rest of the sentence

- ☑ Verbs that help other verbs

You have now learned the tools for using verbs. You can use your knowledge of verbs to write clear and interesting sentences, paragraphs, or stories. There are four other parts of speech. You can use some of the same tools you learned in this book to use these other parts of speech. The chart below shows the other parts of speech and their key features.

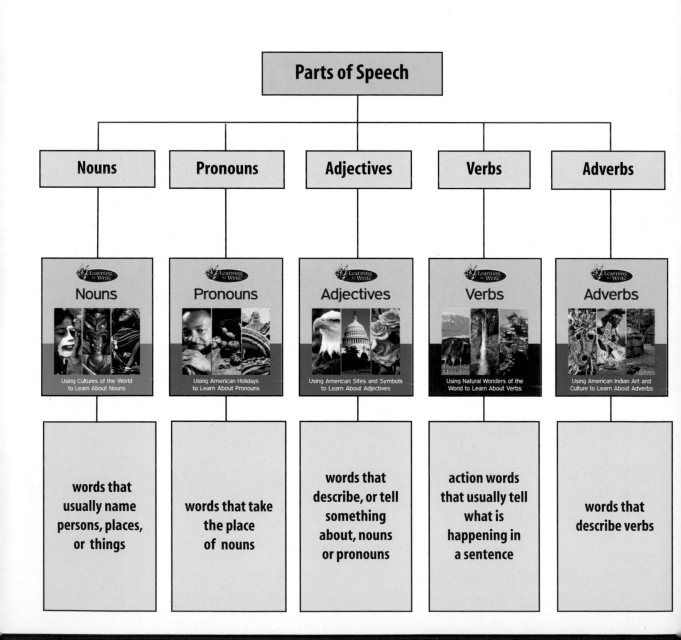

Parts of Speech

Nouns	Pronouns	Adjectives	Verbs	Adverbs
Nouns	Pronouns	Adjectives	Verbs	Adverbs
Using Cultures of the World to Learn About Nouns	Using American Holidays to Learn About Pronouns	Using American Sites and Symbols to Learn About Adjectives	Using Natural Wonders of the World to Learn About Verbs	Using American Indian Art and Culture to Learn About Adverbs
words that usually name persons, places, or things	words that take the place of nouns	words that describe, or tell something about, nouns or pronouns	action words that usually tell what is happening in a sentence	words that describe verbs

Books

Many books provide information on verbs. To learn more about how to use different types of verbs, you can borrow books from the library. To learn more about natural wonders, try reading these books.

Adil, Janeen R. *The Mississippi River*. New York, NY: Weigl Publishers Inc., 2004.

Bekkering, Annalise. *The Great Lakes*. New York, NY: Weigl Publishers Inc., 2009.

Watson, Galadriel. *Mount Kilimanjaro*. New York, NY: Weigl Publishers Inc., 2009.

Websites

On the Internet, you can type terms, such as "verbs" or "types of verbs," into the search bar of your Web browser, and click the search button. It will take you to a number of sites with this information.

Read about more natural wonders at **http://library.thinkquest. org/J002388/naturalwonders.html** and **www.wonderclub .com/AllWorldWonders.html**.

Aboriginal Australians: original people of Australia

being verbs: often called linking verbs because they link the subjects of sentences with information about them

desert: dry, often sandy, region with little rainfall and extreme temperatures

erupts: to break out in a sudden and violent manner

extends: makes longer or wider

extreme: one or two things as different from each other as possible

lava: melted rock that flows from a volcano

noun: the part of speech that is usually used to name a person, place, or thing

pronoun: the part of speech that is used instead of a noun

Index

Amazon rain forest 13, 18
Angel Falls 10, 18

Great Barrier Reef 11, 17, 18
Great Lakes 6, 16, 18

Mauna Loa 7, 18
Mississippi River 5, 18
Mount Everest 8, 9, 18, 19
Mount Kilimanjaro 15, 18, 19

nouns 6, 8, 10, 16, 22

pronouns 6, 8, 10, 16, 22

Sahara Desert 4, 14, 18

verbs, action 6, 8, 9, 12, 13, 14, 15, 18
verbs, helping 6, 12, 13, 14, 15, 18
verbs, linking 6, 10, 11, 12, 14, 15, 18
Victoria Falls 12, 18